gorbachev/yeltsin:

The Fall of Communism

by Stuart A. Kallen

93-94
"109"

Consultant: Margaret Robinson Preska, Ph.D. Russian History
President, Mankato State University [1979-1992]

Published by Abdo & Daughters, 6535 Cecilia Circle, Edina, Minnesota 55439.

Copyright © 1992 by Abdo Consulting Group, Inc., Pentagon Tower, P.O. Box 36036, Minneapolis, Minnesota 55435. International copyrights reserved in all counties. No part of this book may be reproduced in any form without written permission from the publisher. Printed in the United States.

Photo credits: FPG International-cover (Gorbachev)
                   Globe Photos-15
                   UPI/Bettmann-cover (Yeltsin), 5, 6, 7, 10, 20, 23, 27, 31, 33, 37, 48, 53

Edited by: Rosemary Wallner

Library of Congress Cataloging-in-Publication Data

Kallen, Stuart A., 1955-
       Gorbachev/Yeltsin : the fall of communism / written by Stuart A. Kallen ; [edited by Rosemary Wallner].
              p. cm. — (The Rise & fall of the Soviet Union)
       Includes index.
       Summary: Examines the events in the Soviet Union during the time of Gorbachev and Yeltsin, including the failed coup of 1991 and the collapse of the Union itself.
       ISBN 1-56239-105-4 (lib. bdg.)
       1. Soviet Union—History—Attempted coup, 1991—Juvenile literature. 2. Soviet Union—Politics and government—1985-1991—Juvenile literature. 3. Gorbachev, Mikhail Sergeevich, 1931--Juvenile literature. 4. Yeltsin, Boris Nikolayevich, 1931- —Juvenile literature. [1. Soviet Union—History—Attempted coup, 1991. 2. Soviet Union—Politics and government—1985-1991. 3. Gorbachev, Mikhail Sergeevich, 1931- . 4. Yeltsin, Boris Nikolayevich, 1931- .] I. Wallner, Rosemary, 1964- . II. Title. III. Series: Kallen, Stuart A., 1955- Rise & fall of the Soviet Union.
DK292.K35 1992
947.085'4—dc20
                                                                              92-13477
                                                                                   CIP
                                                                                    AC

table of contents

yelling yeltsin

"Yeltsin! Yeltsin! Yeltsin!" The shouts of the Soviet people crackled through the August midnight air like lightning. "Yeltsin! Yeltsin! Yeltsin!" The crowd that had gathered at barricades in front of the "Russian White House" was electrified by the chant. Inside the building, Boris Yeltsin huddled with his advisors. Nearby, in the Soviet Parliament building the grey, dour men who had just overthrown Soviet president Mikhail Gorbachev attempted to gain control. Those shouts of freedom struck terror into their hearts.

Into the crowd stepped Boris Yeltsin, the first freely elected official in Russia since 1918. A man whose childhood was so poverty stricken that all six members of his family had to sleep together on the floor of a one-room apartment with a goat. At the barricades, dozens of hands reached out to lift the white-haired, bear of a man onto a stricken armored car. Yeltsin took control of the small crowd.

Soviet citizens protest, following the ousting
of Soviet President Mikhail Gorbachev.

He announced that a group of men had taken over the government of the Soviet Union and arrested Gorbachev. Yeltsin denounced the coup as illegal and made it perfectly clear that the plotters would face strong resistance in the form of the Soviet people. The coup would fail and freedom would triumph.

Yeltsin's words spread like wildfire though the Soviet capital of Moscow. They crackled through the telephone lines to Leningrad. Within minutes, fax machines, television cameras, and satellites carried Yeltsin's words to an anxious world. Before long, one hundred thousand people had gathered outside of the Russian White House to protect the man who would be their savior, Boris Yeltsin. Those people backed up Yeltsin's words. And he was right — the coup did fail and freedom did win.

the making of history

The term "history in the making" has been used to describe everything from baseball games to rock videos. But the events that took place in the former Soviet Union from August 19 to August 21, 1991, truly revealed the face of history being made.

The Soviet Union, the largest country in the world, ran under a repressive Communist system for seventy-four years. Because of the events started on that August night, the totalitarian system finally came crashing down. The bungled three-day coup was meant to restore the repression. Instead, it cracked Soviet society wide open, giving voice to the angry people who began demanding democracy NOW! The blundering coup plotters could only watch in stone-faced fear as the army and the secret police joined forces with the masses in the street and demanded the return of Yeltsin and Gorbachev to power. The events leading up to this second Russian Revolution are as stunning as the revolution itself.

Leonid Brezhnev lies in state at the House of
Soviets across from the Kremlin.

who's on first?

The president of the Soviet Union was called the General Secretary. When General Secretary Leonid Brezhnev died on November 10, 1982, the fifteen republics of the Soviet Union were left without a visible leader. This was the first death of a General Secretary in office since Joseph Stalin had died in 1953. In a country that holds no elections for the General Secretary, his death caused a great stir within the government. Dozens of men scrambled to get in line for the highest job in Soviet politics. All this was done behind the shield of secrecy. This is why the Communist government has been described in the West as "a riddle wrapped in a mystery inside an enigma."

Brezhnev's health had been terrible for years. He had suffered several strokes and heart attacks; doctors declared him clinically dead twice. Wherever the doddering old Communist went, an emergency medical team and an ambulance followed. Brezhnev's staff had hidden his progressive sickness from the citizens with a steady stream of propaganda.

By the end of the Brezhnev era, however, the Soviet Union enjoyed some of the best years that country had ever experienced. Living standards were up and there were more private automobiles, restaurants, and luxury goods. And the Soviet Union had achieved military equality with the United States for the first time. Moscow's influence in other countries went beyond the wildest dreams of early Soviet leaders. Laos, Cambodia, Ethiopia, Angola, Mozambique, and other countries were all either run by Communists or were pro-Soviet.

When Brezhnev died, the military was put on full alert. The day after his death, Moscow looked like an armed camp. The secret police (KGB) and the army set up roadblocks and checkpoints along every road. No one could go near the Kremlin, the headquarters of Soviet government. The first person to learn of Brezhnev's death was Yuri Andropov, the head of the KGB. Because of the power of the dreaded KGB, Andropov was expected to take Brezhnev's place as General Secretary. But a vicious political battle developed between Andropov and Brezhnev's chief of staff, Konstantin Chernenko.

The next day, the city of Moscow ground to a halt. Soldiers, policemen, and KGB agents stood three abreast throughout the city. The three-hundred-member Central Committee, the Soviet Congress, huddled in the Kremlin all day. When it was over, it was announced that Yuri Andropov would be the new Soviet General Secretary. Chernenko was demoted and ignored by the new government.

andropov's new vision

Soon, the masses of Soviet people saw their new leader for the first time. From behind the mysterious walls of the Kremlin, Yuri Andropov stepped into the bright lights of the world press. He was a direct man who readily admitted he had no immediate solutions for Soviet problems. But he surrounded himself with intellectuals, scientists, and journalists. After the stale, stodgy years of Brezhnev, most people felt happy about their new leader. They felt that the future held promise.

Andropov remained a mystery to the world while he was in power. He seemed to be a man made of contradictions. He wrote romantic poetry to his wife while running the world's most brutal police organization. The dark veil of the KGB cloaked him in secrecy. His chronic kidney ailment was a state secret. But Andropov was the first Soviet leader to admit that strict Communist ideology would never bring the Soviet Union into the modern world.

President Yuri Andropov, who succeeded
Brezhnev in 1982, was formerly the head of the KGB.

new nukes and shoot downs

Andropov had more than domestic problems to trouble him. Soviet relations with the United States had reached all-time lows. United States President Ronald Reagan decided to place medium-range nuclear missiles in Europe. Those Pershing Two missiles were pointed straight at Moscow. This was to counteract the Soviet nuclear submarines that plied the waters near the East Coast of the United States. Reagan also called the Soviet Union the "Evil Empire" in speeches. The Soviet press described Reagan as "a power-thirsty lunatic about to blow up the world." Such huffing and puffing by the world's superpowers made front page news all over the world. The Soviets reacted by threatening to put new missiles in Eastern Europe. They also threatened to assume a "launch on warning" posture, meaning that computers would launch Soviet missiles instantly if the Soviets perceived a threat. The specter of nuclear annihilation loomed larger than ever before.

On September 1, 1983, a Soviet jet fighter pilot shot down a Korean Air Lines (KAL) passenger jet that had accidentally strayed over the Soviet Union. Experts say that the pilot who did the shooting should have known that the KAL jet was a passenger plane instead of a spy plane. Through error or bad intent, the plane was shot down, killing 269 persons including more than fifty Americans and a congressman. Tensions between the United States and the Soviet Union rose to record levels.

Bereaved families cast bouquets into the sea
to mourn victims of the KAL jetliner downed 9/1/83

andropov drops off

hile this war of nerves was being played out, Andropov lay in the hospital. He had been gravely ill, and one of his kidneys had been removed. Although the average Soviet citizen did not know it, Andropov was a dying man. As in Brezhnev's case, Soviet television pieced together old film footage of Andropov to give the impression that he was healthy and in control. Meanwhile, Mikhail Gorbachev was doing a fine job covering Andropov's duties.

After disappearing from the public for 175 days, Andropov died on February 10, 1984.

On February 14, on a frigid winter day, a huge state funeral was held outdoors for Yuri Andropov. By then, Konstantin Chernenko had been named General Secretary of the Soviet Union. While Chernenko had lost the power battle with Andropov only fifteen months before, he was now there to fill the dead man's shoes.

As Chernenko gave his speech at the funeral, it was obvious to everyone that another sick, dying man had been made General Secretary. Gorbachev had been the obvious choice for the job. But Andropov had not gotten rid of enough of the old men who had supported Brezhnev. The old guard still held enough power to install Chernenko as General Secretary. Chernenko was the last gasp of the old guard — the old generation against the new. And he slurred his words and wheezed in the frigid air that day, mumbling phony compliments about the dead Andropov.

the old still holds

Konstantin Chernenko was a man with no special qualities or virtues. At the age of seventy-two, he was the oldest man in Soviet history to become General Secretary. But Chernenko was Brezhnev's closest aide for thirty years. This was good enough for the old men in the Kremlin.

A sense of gloom settled over the Soviet people who had been promised positive change under Andropov. Even the propagandists could find little good to say about Chernenko. Those who knew him described him as a "tremendously average man."

Chernenko filled his official duties in a manner that was painful to watch. His nationally televised appearances showed a man moving with difficulty. His eyes were glazed and he was obviously in pain. His struggle gained him sympathy from people who disliked him. They saw an old and sick man bravely filling his patriotic duty with dignity. After thirteen months of pushing Brezhnev's tired old policies, Konstantin Chernenko died on March 10, 1985.

This was the third death of a General Secretary in as many years.

In typical Soviet fashion, Chernenko's death was not immediately announced. Instead, Moscow radio played mellow classical music to "calm the people." March 12 brought the death announcement — after twelve hours of funeral dirges on radio and television. Four hours later, Mikhail Gorbachev was the new General Secretary of the Soviet Union.

the changing of the guard

In December 1984, months before Chernenko's death, Mikhail Gorbachev visited Great Britain. There, he became the focus of the Western media. After that, it was obvious that the Soviet Union had a new leader who possessed charm, poise, and intelligence. Under the bright lights of the press, Gorbachev appeared as a man in control. To help matters, Gorbachev was accompanied by his wife, Raisa. From the moment she stepped off the airplane, the press swooned over her natural charm, beauty, and intelligence. It was obvious that the couple represented a new Soviet generation who talked, dressed, and behaved in a way that Westerners could understand. The image of the frowning, mean, old Soviet dictator was swept away.

Gorbachev did not seem to be a power-hungry man. At one time, he told a close friend, "Can you believe that there is a person who would want to become general secretary at this time?" This remark reflects on the massive problems that the Soviet Union was facing.

There were shortages of everything, from food and clothing to housing. Those shortages had gotten even worse in recent years. Average Soviet citizens spend one-third of their lives waiting in lines at shops. Shoppers sometimes do not know what might be for sale at the end of the line, but they will buy it anyway. If they don't need it they can trade it for something else.

In 1985, those people had been waiting for something more important than shoes, TV sets, and toasters. They had been waiting for freedom, democracy, free speech, and the right to travel, worship, and live as they pleased. If Gorbachev was to complete the mission that he made for himself, he would have to reform Soviet agriculture, industry, education, housing, politics, and society from the top down.

Gorbachev plunged into his new job with his sleeves rolled up, ready for action and purpose. His activism made good television, and he was the first Soviet leader with an instant television personality. He was embarrassed by the Soviet propaganda machinery that had elevated every other leader to a god-like status. He told newspaper editors that he did not want to be quoted constantly as a fountain of wisdom.

He disliked the empty patriotic slogans and sugar-coated news that had been the stock in trade of the Soviet press for seventy years.

More importantly, Gorbachev ordered physical examinations for all the top Soviet officials. Many of the top figures in the Kremlin were eighty or ninety years old. Gorbachev wanted it known that he needed healthy and vigorous people in charge. Gorbachev amazed people when he spent days touring Moscow schools, factories, hospitals, supermarkets, and apartments. He even went down into the streets where he was mobbed by people wanting to shake his hand and tell them their problems. On television he echoed the average people's complaints about food shortages, shoddy consumer goods, and poor services. No Soviet leader had ever taken responsibility for — or even mentioned — the system's failings.

Gorbachev's first year in office was described by a Russian word meaning "reconstruction" or "rebuilding." That word — perestroyka — was also defined as "a major transformation of the mind." Gorbachev ushered in a new era in Soviet history, in which the themes were honesty, openness, less talk, and more action. Once the people experienced perestroyka, there was no turning back.

day of the disaster

orbachev's one year honeymoon with the Soviet people ended on April 26, 1986. On that day, a sudden surge of electricity touched off an explosion at the Chernobyl nuclear power plant in the Ukraine. The talkative Gorbachev remained silent for eight days as a cloud of toxic radiation spewed across Europe. At first, the Soviets refused to admit the disaster had happened at all. This followed the old Soviet passion for secrecy that has covered up dozens of other disasters. Gorbachev finally admitted that the disaster had happened eighteen days later on Soviet television.

When Chernobyl blew, flames shot one hundred feet in the air while scattered radioactive fragments settled on nearby towns. For ten days, the radioactive plume wafted out over Lithuania, Poland, Sweden, Norway, Germany, the Netherlands, and Belgium.

After the Chernobyl accident, helicopters with radiation counters stayed in the air for days.

Plant operators told officials in Moscow what had happened but the officials could not understand the scope of the disaster. The press was not notified and neither were any of the countries who were in the path of the radiation. Thirty-one workers died in the accident and hospitals treated two hundred more for radiation sickness. Eventually, 100,000 people were evacuated from the area. The effects of the radiation will be felt by the people and the environment for decades to come.

The world press scolded Gorbachev for failing to come forward immediately with news of the accident. The disaster was not only an environmental one, but a public relations disaster as well. People began to question if they could trust Gorbachev.

the wall falls down

The late eighties saw Gorbachev busy signing arms treaties with the United States and allowing new freedoms in the Soviet Union. The move to openness, called glasnost continued on its rocky path. Ironically, when people were given the right to criticize the government, they attacked Gorbachev, the man who had given them that freedom. The Baltic republics of Lithuania, Latvia, and Estonia had been demanding independence for years. Gorbachev was forced to send in Soviet troops to stop demonstrations in the streets. For a while, it looked like Gorbachev was going back to the brutal policies of his predecessors. Then, in November 1989, the eyes of the world experienced history being made in Eastern Europe.

Communism was forced onto Eastern Europe after World War II. Some people in countries like Czechoslovakia, Yugoslavia, Poland, East Germany, Hungary, and Romania supported the Soviet-backed governments. But nowhere were the Communists a majority.

Joseph Stalin was willing to use brute force to make believers out of the Eastern Europeans. He never succeeded. These countries always considered the Soviet-installed governments alien. Only the fear of a Soviet invasion kept the satellite countries in line. Communism counted on fear. People who spoke out could lose their house, job, car, and even their life. When people in Hungary tried to throw off the reigns of Communist rule in 1956, the Soviet Red Army brutally shot them in the streets. Twenty-five thousand died. In 1968, Czechoslovakia tried the same thing with less casualties but the same tragic results.

When glasnost appeared on the horizon, the cold Communist rule of Eastern Europe began to thaw. Gorbachev stressed each country should have a right to find its own path. No longer would Soviet tanks idled on the borders of these countries, waiting to attack dissenters. In 1989, a wave of revolution swept across Eastern Europe. This revolution was not aimed at reforming Communism. The new aim was to install democratically elected officials in a capitalist system.

It started in September, with a trickle of young East Germans fleeing their country to the west via Czechoslovakia, Hungary, and Poland. The trickle turned into a flood by October. A staggering two hundred people an hour fled the repressive regime of Erich Honecker in East Germany. On October 7, Gorbachev appeared in East Germany to celebrate the fortieth birthday of Soviet rule there. Protesters in the street chanted "Gorby! Gorby! We need freedom!" With the whole world watching, Honecker's police force celebrated the anniversary by clubbing the protesters with riot sticks. Eleven days later, Honecker was removed from power.

On November 7, 1989, Honecker's replacement, Egon Krenz, opened the East German border for the first time in nearly thirty years. People the world over were treated to the spectacle of thousands of people gleefully dancing on the hated Berlin Wall. Wide-eyed East Germans saw the incredible array of food, clothes, electronics, and autos when they went shopping in West Germany. To people who had been denied such basic necessities as food, soap, and shoes, this was quite an experience.

On November 9, 1989, tens of thousands of people gathered at the Berlin Wall in East Germany.

A big section of the wall is lifted out by a crane as East Germany starts to dismantle the Berlin Wall

That wall had been built in 1961 to keep people from leaving that Communist country. Hundreds of people had been shot trying to escape to the West. But that night in November, the wall was torn down by the people. Before the night was over, the divided Germany was reunited. Gorbachev decided not to send in the tanks, and all across Eastern Europe the walls of Communism came crashing down with incredible speed. Governments that had been in place for forty years vanished overnight.

Gorbachev did not engineer the events that led to the collapse of the Soviet empire, but he had set the whole process in motion. In a mere six weeks, Joseph Stalin's dream of a Communist empire across Eastern Europe lay in tatters. Soon the Revolution spread to the Soviet Union itself.

hijacking soviet democracy

While the Eastern European countries struggled with their new-found freedoms, the Soviet Union was cracking up. The Soviet Union was the largest country in the world because it was made up of fifteen republics, or states. This was indicated in the country's formal name, the Union of Soviet Socialist Republics, or U.S.S.R. Many of these socialist republics, such as Lithuania were only part of the U.S.S.R. because they were forced to be. When the countries of Eastern Europe gained their independence, most of the Soviet republics demanded the same. But most of the republics are dependent on each other. Some specialize in farming and food production, others specialize in steel and industry, others in mining and natural resources. The central authority in the Kremlin tried to coordinate and distribute all the means of production. This has proven to be an impossible task in such a huge country. That is why massive shortages have dogged the Soviet Union since its founding.

On August 20, 1991, Gorbachev was to sign a historic treaty between the fifteen republics. The treaty would transfer many powers (including those over taxes, natural resources, and state security) to the republics. After seventy-four years, the Kremlin would no longer control the republics through threats and intimidation. The Treaty on the Union of the Sovereign States would also allow the republics to freely elect their own officials. If that happened, many of the Kremlin's old-guard bureaucrats would have lost their jobs full of privilege and wealth.

This treaty would have made Mikhail Gorbachev a world hero — the man who gave democracy to three hundred million people. But before the treaty was signed, Gorbachev needed a vacation. He needed time to relax with his family and ponder the great deed he was about to perform. He needed some peace from the intense political battle he was waging in the name of democracy.

The Crimea is a peninsula in Russia that juts into the Black Sea. It has been a vacation spot for Soviets for generations. From the top leaders at the Kremlin to the workers in the steel mills, a Crimean vacation is considered a must.

On Sunday, August 18, Gorbachev relaxed with Raisa and his grandchildren at his Crimean vacation home. Gorbachev had worked until 4 p.m. on the speech he would give at the signing of the treaty on Tuesday. At ten minutes to five, his chief body guard informed him that a group of people wanted to see him. Who were they, asked Gorbachev, and why had they been let into the house? Gorbachev reached for the phone. It was dead. He tried a second phone, then a third, then a fourth. All dead. Suddenly Gorbachev realized that he had been taken prisoner in his own home.

Gorbachev quickly rounded up his family and warned them of what was happening. When he returned to his office, five men stood there. They were all top-ranking Kremlin leaders and generals. They demanded that Gorbachev sign a decree proclaiming an emergency and turning all of his power over to the Vice President, Gennadi Yanayev. Gorbachev's reply: "Get lost!"

By then, a special detachment of KGB guards had surrounded the vacation home. In case Gorbachev somehow escaped and tried to return to Moscow, the KGB parked tractors across the runway of the nearby airport.

That way, Gorbachev's presidential jet could not take off. More than twelve hours passed before the world knew of the Soviet coup. But at 6 a.m. Monday morning, the Soviet news agency, TASS, falsely reported that Gorbachev was sick and had yielded his powers to Yanayev. An hour later, TASS announced that an eight-man committee called the State Committee for the State of Emergency would rule the country.

The eight men on the Emergency Committee set up the machinery for a dictatorship. All newspapers were ordered to stop publishing, except for nine pro-coup sheets. Political parties were outlawed and protest demonstrations banned. Muscovites going to work that morning saw troops, tanks, and armored personnel carriers cordoning off streets and seizing key installations.

The men who seized control also tried to buy off the people. Liquor stores were thrown wide open as huge crowds gathered to snap up the vodka that had been in such short supply for the past five years. The men plotting the coup figured that a drunk populous was a happy populous.

bumbling plotters

Free vodka or not, it was obvious early on that the coup attempt was half-hearted. The plotters had failed to follow the basic rules of any successful coup. First, they failed to arrest popular leaders who could organize resistance. Boris Yeltsin — probably the most popular leader the Soviet Union has ever had — was not arrested. Other leaders who backed democracy were free to organize protests in most Soviet republics.

The second mistake of the coup plotters was their failure to pull the plug on the communications of anyone except Gorbachev. In the days before mass communications this would have been easier. But the eighties brought fax machines, computers, video cameras, and cellular phones to the Soviet Union as elsewhere. Western leaders and the press were amazed at the outpouring of information on these high-tech machines. Using computer networks and fax machines, people in many big cities were mobilized to protest within hours.

Probably the biggest failure of the Emergency Committee was their lack of reliable soldiers. The plotters used troops and equipment that happened to be on hand. The soldiers had only a vague idea of what was happening and how they were supposed to react. Some soldiers in Moscow thought that they were in some sort of odd parade or drill. And the soldiers were immediately over-whelmed by the people in the streets. Thousands of people stood face to face with the armed soldiers, shouting at them to go home and worse. By that point, only a massive bloodbath could have insured the success of the coup.

the turning point

At 12:30 p.m. Monday, Boris Yeltsin clamored on top of an armored truck outside the Russian White House. He denounced the coup and called for a general strike to thwart it. Yeltsin made it clear that the people would resist the coup at every step. His appearance helped inspire protesters throughout the Soviet Union. Although this was the turning point, few realized it at the time.

Yeltsin's fiery speech was only heard by about two hundred people. But as the word spread, the crowd grew and grew. Soon tens of thousands of people gathered around the White House protecting the man inside who would lead them to freedom — Boris Yeltsin.

At 5 p.m. on Monday, the plotters called a press conference to introduce themselves. Instead of coming across like a take-charge group, the men appeared nervous and sorry, and the press conference was a disaster. They gave an unbelievable excuse for the coup, saying Gorbachev was too tired and ill to run the country.

They falsely said that what they had done was perfectly legal according to Soviet law. And they claimed ridiculously that they would continue reform. The men were sniffling, scratching, and shaking. Gorbachev later stated, "They said I was sick, but they were the ones whose hands were shaking."

Gorbachev was hunkered down at his vacation home. He followed the earth-shaking events on old, worn radios that his men had found in the basement. Ironically, he was getting his information from Radio Liberty and Voice of America — signals from two networks that the Soviet Union had jammed for years. In fact, it had been illegal to listen to these stations — which gave a mix of music, news, and Western propaganda — in the Soviet Union. Besides listening to the radio, Gorbachev made four videotapes to prove that he was not sick at all. Raisa was terrified by the experience. She later had to be treated for what amounted to a nervous breakdown.

blood in the streets

By Tuesday, August 20, the day that the treaty was to have been signed, all of the Western nations condemned the coup. They stated that there would be no normal relations with the Soviet Union until the rightful government was returned. They also cut off the economic aid that the country desperately needed. Coal miners in Siberia refused to work. Resolutions condemning the Emergency Committee were passed in cities from one end of the Soviet Union to the other. The streets were filled with protesters. In the streets of Moscow, 150,000 people chanted, "We will win!" Yeltsin made a bold speech while dozens of men held bullet-proof shields up around him.

By Tuesday night, it was obvious that the coup would fail without the use of deadly force. As a hard rain poured from the sky, loudspeakers blared warnings that tanks and troops were rolling toward the Russian White House.

Sixty airplanes filled with paratroopers prepared for an armed assault. Thousands of people in the streets worked through the night to build barricades to thwart the tanks. Thousands of people bravely locked arms to form a human chain around the building. Hundreds of men came forward to lay down their lives to protect the building. As they trooped in, a priest read them the Lord's Prayer.

At a quarter past midnight, a live report broadcast on Radio Liberty said that there had been some short bursts of gunfire near the White House. The radio said that armored cars and trucks had tried to crash the front-line barricades. Soon one...two...three people lay crushed dead in the street.

One man, a veteran from the Afghan war, was shot in the head when he climbed up on an armored car to talk with the soldiers. Another man was run over when he tried to remove the body of the first victim. Then the vehicle was set on fire. When the army crew abandoned the burning car to hide in another one, they shot randomly over their heads. That is when the third man was killed. Several hours later it was reported that the armored car was not attacking the White House.

The soldiers had run into the barricades by mistake while on patrol and had gotten nervous. The blood was spilled by soldiers not acting on orders, but on fear. Fortunately, these were the only casualties of the Moscow coup.

the rockin' ending

Some soldiers sent to menace the White House decided to protect it instead. One top general ordered his troops to defend Yeltsin. Soon many other top military men sided with Yeltsin. On Wednesday morning, the plotters tried their last futile moves. They seized control of several radio and TV stations in Lithuania and Moscow. But by 2:15 p.m. Yeltsin announced that some of the coup leaders were running for the airport to get out of town. They were chased down and arrested. The Defense Ministry ordered all troops to clear out of Moscow and his order was happily obeyed.

The crowd cheered as the soldiers, some waving revolutionary flags, rode atop their armored cars on the way out of town. The order to clear out had come from Gorbachev. For two days he had demanded to use the phone and return to Moscow. On Wednesday, he was suddenly allowed to use the phone. He called the defense minister and gave the orders.

Gorbachev had given the orders, but what really defeated the coup were the people of Moscow. They were the ones who had put their bodies in front of the tanks and the guns. Western rock-and-roll music — which wasn't even allowed in the Soviet Union until the mid-1980's — had also done a lot to spread the message of freedom to Soviet youth. So it was very appropriate that when the coup failed, one of the first things heard over Moscow radio was a message from Mick Jagger of the Rolling Stones. Jagger said, "I fully support the brave and defiant actions of the defenders of the Russian parliament building and other groups throughout the Soviet Union, in defending their right to choose their own leadership and way of life. We're on your side, and we're rooting for you." Messages from former Beatle Ringo Starr and the Eurythmics' Dave Stewart followed shortly.

After the coup, a party started at the barricades. A loudspeaker system was set up on the stairs of the White House and Soviet rock bands started a spontaneous "Rock on the Barricades" concert.

Within hours of the failed coup, a crowd of thousands gathered outside the KGB headquarters in Moscow. One of the most forbidding places in Soviet imagination, the interrogation rooms and cells beneath the building were the sight of terror and torture for millions. The nerve of the crowd strengthened and cheers went up as the statue of KGB founder, "Iron Felix" Dzherzhinsky, tumbled to the ground. In the rest of the country statues of other Soviet leaders, including its founder Vladimir Lenin, toppled into the dust. Without the terror of the KGB and the propaganda of the Communist Party, the people of the Soviet Union would be free to follow their own paths, wherever they may lead.

Meanwhile, several members of the failed coup boarded a plane and went to find Gorbachev. It is not clear whether they were going to beg his forgiveness or kill him (they were carrying guns). Complicated security arrangements were made to return Gorbachev to Moscow.

At 2:15 a.m. on Thursday, Gorbachev stepped off of his plane looking haggard and tired. He flashed his famous smile and the world breathed a little easier.

The men who had plotted the coup were rounded up and arrested. One man committed suicide before he could be found. Dozens of other people who sided with the coup plotters were either arrested or forced to resign. The charge against these men was treason. The punishment is the death penalty.

For three days, one of the world's two superpowers careened out of control. Eight men stepped out of the shadows of the Kremlin to take control of the Soviet Union, its four-million-man army, and 30,000 nuclear warheads. When the coup crashed, almost seventy-five years of Communist rule dissolved into dust. Much of the dust settled on Mikhail Gorbachev who was blamed for surrounding himself with men such as the plotters. Although he survived the coup, his power and popularity sunk to an all-time low. Out of the dust rose Boris Yeltsin who Gorbachev forced out of the Communist Party in 1987. During the coup, Yeltsin made a comeback and became one of the most powerful men in the Soviet Union.

Although they were fierce rivals, Gorbachev and Yeltsin had to work together to raise the Soviet Union out of the dust.

the end of an empire

n the weeks following the coup, every Soviet republic tugged in different directions. Gorbachev offered his vision of the future. He argued, in vain, for preservation of something much like the old Soviet Union. Its collapse, he warned, "threatens the lives and property of millions of people. We do not have a right to make a mistake of this proportion."

Meanwhile, the Soviet troubles did not stop. Inflation ran at 1,000 percent. Food shortages threatened massive starvation without the help of the United States. Just getting the food to every town and village was an impressive task because of the country's old and broken-down transportation system.

Robbers, murderers, and other criminals ran wild because of the breakdown of the KGB and other police forces. Ancient ethnic rivalries between cultures threatened civil war in some republics. And Soviet nuclear weapons that were spread out all over the huge country could spell disaster if they fell into the wrong hands.

environmental nightmares

Pollution from inefficient, out-dated factories built in the 1930's threaten the health and well being of Soviet citizens and the entire planet. Air pollution in one hundred cities is ten times worse than standards allow. Only one third of Soviet sewage is treated, the rest is dumped into rivers. Toxins fill the sky and once-beautiful rivers are open sewers. Ninety percent of the Black Sea is biologically dead. In a country of constant food shortages, fish harvests are down by two thirds. Pesticides contaminate thirty percent of the food, causing 14,000 deaths and 700,000 illnesses each year. Many of the Soviet Union's nuclear power plants have the same design as the one that exploded at Chernobyl. In a country desperately short of electricity, it is impossible to shut these power plants down.

Billions of scarce dollars are needed to clean up these environmental disasters. Thousands of jobs will be lost if the factories are shut down.

With Moscow's power weakened, cleaning up these environmental nightmares will prove to be a difficult task.

a global peace

ithout a doubt, the best thing to come from the Soviet crack-up was the easing of tensions between the Soviet Union and the United States. With the threat of nuclear war greatly diminished, United States President George Bush ordered the dismantling of thousands of nuclear weapons. The Soviets, too, were ready to melt down many nuclear weapons. Bush also ordered the United States military to "stand down" from their nuclear alert. That meant that for the first time in over forty years, the United States and the Soviet Union did not have their armies poised over nuclear weapons, ready to launch at a moment's notice.

While there were still thousands of long-ranged nuclear missiles, those steps took the world many steps back from nuclear disaster.

bye-bye, gorby

On December 8, 1991, the republics of Russia, Ukraine, and Byelorussia formed a commonwealth. The republics declared the government of the Soviet Union dead. Soon, other Soviet republics joined the new commonwealth. On December 25, under pressure from Yeltsin and others, Mikhail Gorbachev resigned as General Secretary of the Soviet Union. In his farewell speech, Gorbachev said, "We are now living in a new world." He said that he would "discontinue his activities" as president.

The Soviet regime passed into history at age seventy-four. The collapse was so swift and complete, that many countries wondered why the Soviet Union had frightened them for so long.

Gorbachev had set his people on the road to freedom seven years earlier. Now he had become an object of ridicule and scorn. All the problems created with the crack-up of the country were laid at Gorbachev's door.

The Soviet Union became the Commonwealth of Independent States. Boris Yeltsin, Russia's president, put sweeping changes into place that shook the entire commonwealth. His first major reform was to remove the system of artificial price controls that had governed the price of everything from salt to refrigerators for seven decades.

On January 2, 1992, when the price controls were removed, the price of everything skyrocketed. The price of sausage went from five rubles a pound to fifty-four rubles a pound. Smoked bacon, which hadn't been seen for two years, cost 550 rubles a pound. The average citizen does not make that much in a month. Massive food shortages sparked riots in the streets. Outside Moscow, whole areas lacked water and electricity. Thousands of angry people held rallies demanding that Yeltsin resign and the old Communist system be reinstated.

Meanwhile, in the republic of Georgia, war broke out. The elected leader of that republic barricaded himself in the Parliament building. Armed militia battled over control in the streets. Hundreds were killed as the president was driven into exile in Armenia. When supporters of the Georgian president rallied to support him, opposition soldiers shot them. They left the Georgian Parliament building a smoking ruin.

There were troubles in the other republics as well. Ukraine and Russia fought over ownership of the Soviet Black Sea fleet, docked in Ukraine. Those ships were the most advanced nuclear submarines and battleships in the Soviet fleet. Tajikistan announced that it would seize a secret plant in its territory and try to sell nuclear technology to Arab countries. And 27,000 nuclear warheads were still spread throughout the former Soviet Union. Boris Yeltsin said that they would no longer be pointed at the United States. But they were a wildcard in a very dangerous game of nuclear poker.

To stave off another revolution, President Bush and forty-two other countries promised billions of dollars in aid to the wounded republics.

the year zero

The Commonwealth of Indepedent States started again at the year zero. Never before has such a mighty nation of so many different cultures dissolved with such rapid speed. The lives of almost three hundred million people hung in the balance. Nothing and everything was tried to solve the country's massive problems. From the Arctic tundra of Siberia to the deserts of Azerbaijan, from the European cities of Lithuania, to the Asian cultures of Kirghizia, the Soviet Union was an experiment in human diversity.

If the peoples of this world ever want to exist in peace and harmony, the Commonwealth of Independent States may be the book from which we all will learn in the future. We know that the breakup of the Soviet Union has lead to a greater peace between the superpowers. Now we can only hope that it leads to peace within the Commonwealth itself.

glossary

annex — To add a state or country into another country. Joseph Stalin annexed the republic of Georgia into the Soviet Union in 1922 making it part of the Soviet Union.

capitalism — An economic system where individuals own goods and where prices, production, and distribution are determined by competition in a free market. The United States is a capitalist country.

coup — A sudden overturn of power when one person or group replaces another as leader of a country.

democracy — A form of government in which people vote for their leaders in a free election. The United States is a democracy.

dictatorship — A form of government where all power is given to one person or a small group of people. The citizens in a dictatorship have no choice in who rules their country. The Soviet Union was a dictatorship until 1991.

General Secretary — Title given to the leader of the Soviet Union.

ideology — A set of beliefs that guides an individual, group, or culture.

Kremlin — A fortified building in Moscow that contains the government center of the Soviet Union. Also the name used for the entire Soviet government.

index